This book is given

From:

On this day:

Pray at all times.

Romans 12:12 ICB

365 Talks with JESUS

Prayers to Share with Little Ones

Amy Parker

PUBLISHING GROUP

Brentwood, Tennessee

Text Copyright © 2024 by B&H Publishing Group
Illustrations by Sally Garland, Copyright © 2023 by B&H Publishing Group
Published by B&H Publishing Group, Brentwood, Tennessee
All rights reserved. ISBN: 978-1-0877-8714-5
Unless otherwise noted, all Scripture quotations are taken from the
Christian Standard Bible®, Copyright © 2017 by Holman Bible Publishers.
Used by permission. Christian Standard Bible® and CSB® are
federally registered trademarks of Holman Bible Publishers.
Scripture quotations marked ICB are taken from the
International Children's Bible® Copyright© 1986, 1988, 1999, 2015
by Thomas Nelson. Used by permission.
Scripture quotations marked NIV are taken from the New International
Version®, NIV® Copyright ©1973, 1978, 1984, 2011 by Biblica, Inc.®
Used by permission. All rights reserved worldwide.
Dewey Decimal Classification: CE
Subject Heading: PRAYERS / PRAYER / PARENT-CHILD-RELATIONSHIP
Printed in Shenzhen, Guangdong, China, September 2023
1 2 3 4 5 6 · 28 27 26 25 24

To all my readers,
whatever your age, may you
never stop talking to Jesus

Dear Parent,

This little book is a collection of 365 simple, Bible-based prayers to spark conversations between your little ones and Jesus. We believe prayer—seeking Jesus every day, in every way—is the most transformational tool with which we can empower our children. And the earlier we start, the better.

We have carefully written these prayers to be relatable to preschoolers, in language they can understand. Each short prayer can be read aloud by the parent and includes a quick, bold line for your child to repeat before saying, "Amen."

We've organized the prayers into categories so that you can help your child find helpful words to pray when they need it most. Of course, you can also read through the book in order.

Either way, our prayer is that these little prayers spark big conversations between little hearts and the One who knows them best and loves them the most. And in doing so, we pray that your little ones build an instinctual response of running to Him freely, casting their cares on Him, because He cares for them (1 Peter 5:7).

Praying for you,
Amy Parker

Talks with Jesus . . .

When I Am
HAPPY

"Let your light shine."—Jesus
Matthew 5:16

Dear Jesus,

You've told us to let our light shine (Matthew 5:16). Help me always to let my light shine for You. I want the whole world to be happy. I want the whole world to find joy in You. **Jesus, help me to shine so that the world will know You. Amen.**

Jesus,

Today I am happy because
_____. Thank You! And
thank You for all the little things
and big things that make me happy.
**Help me to remember that every
good thing comes from You.
Amen.**

Hi Jesus,

You have given me so many people who love me. I have people who take care of me. They cook yummy food for me. They teach me important things. They tuck me in at night. **Thank You, Jesus, for people who love me. Amen.**

Dear Jesus,

Just knowing that You are with me makes me happy. I love singing songs about You. I love reading about You. I love talking to You. **Thank You for bringing so much joy! Amen.**

Dear Jesus,

You give us the sun to shine down rays of happiness. It makes the flowers grow. It spills through the windows of my home. It warms my face, and I know it's shining even with my eyes closed. **Thank You, Jesus, for the sunshine to warm my days. Amen.**

Wow, Jesus!

You amaze me. When I think of all You've done and all that You are, I am so happy to know that You're listening to me and that You love me. **Thank You, Jesus, for all that You are. Amen.**

Dear Jesus,

On rainy days, boring days, and even kind of scary days, I can find joy in You. I can splash in puddles. I can enjoy the quiet. I can trust You are with me. **Thank You, Jesus, for being my joy, no matter what. Amen.**

Dear Jesus,

Thank You so much for playtime. Thank You for letting me jump and run and roll and slide. Moving makes my body healthy and my heart happy. **Thank You, Jesus, for knowing that I need playtime. Amen.**

Dear Jesus,

The Bible reminds us to help others
(Hebrews 13:16). Thank You for this
reminder. Sometimes it can be hard,
but helping other people makes me
so happy. And it makes them happy
too! **Please show me how to help
the people around me. Amen.**

Hi Jesus,

This day was long and busy. But it makes me happy to think about everything I did today. I learned big, played big, and loved big. **Thank You, Jesus, for fun, full days. Amen.**

Dear Jesus,

The Bible reminds us that we are happy when we trust in You (Proverbs 16:20). It helps me feel safe and loved to know that You are always there. Thank You for being someone I can count on. **Help me always to know that I can trust in You. Amen.**

Dear Jesus,

I know that following You helps me to be happy. Your rules keep me safe, and Your words help me make the best choices. Thank You for showing me the best way to live. **Help me, Jesus, to follow You. Amen.**

Jesus,

When I snuggle in to sleep at night, I know that You're watching over me. It makes me feel so safe and peaceful and calm. My family can all rest well knowing that You are watching us as we sleep. **Thank You, Jesus, for watching over me. Amen.**

Dear Jesus,

Thank You for all my friends. I am so happy to have friends to play with, learn with, grow with, and love. **Jesus, please take care of my friends and show me how to take care of them too. Amen.**

Hi Jesus,

Today I am so happy. But I know that some people are sad. Some people are hurting. Some people are lonely. Please help them, Jesus. And show me how to help them too. **Jesus, please be with those who are sad. Amen.**

Dear Jesus,

I look around and see so many things You've given me that make me happy. I want to share those things and that joy with everyone around me. **Jesus, help me to share the happiness You've given me with the world. Amen.**

Jesus,

I know that to be truly happy, I need to know You. Help me, Jesus. Help me to keep learning about the Bible, talking to You, and growing more like You. **Help me to know You better, Jesus. Amen.**

Dear Jesus,

We have so many reasons to be happy. You gave us a beautiful world. We have flowers. We have birds and puppies. We have butterflies. And most of all, we have You. **Thank You, Jesus, for everything. Amen.**

When I Am
SAD

"Blessed are those who mourn, for they will be comforted."—Jesus

Matthew 5:4

Dear Jesus,

Your Word, the Bible, tells us that people who "mourn" (those who are sad) will be blessed. It says they will be comforted (Matthew 5:4). I'm very thankful You promise to cheer us up and comfort us. **Please help me to feel better when I am sad, Jesus. Amen.**

Jesus,

I am sad today because
_____. Can You help me
understand these things? Please
help these things to get better.
Please help me remember that You
are in control of everything. **Jesus,
I trust in You. Amen.**

Dear Jesus,

I know that You are powerful. I know that You made me, and You have known me from the very beginning. I know that You made me to have all kinds of feelings— feelings like sadness and happiness and excitement and anger. **Thank You for caring about how I feel, Jesus. Amen.**

Dear Jesus,

Sometimes I get sad or mad or grumpy. When I do, will You help me remember all the gifts You've given me? Remind me of all the things that make me happy. **Jesus, please help me remember all the reasons I have to smile. Amen.**

Jesus,

Sometimes when my mind and body are tired, they can make me cry. I know that my mind and body need rest. Thank You for giving us feelings to remind us of what we need. **Help me to get the rest I need, Jesus. Amen.**

Dear Jesus,

The Bible tells us that even You, the Son of God, got sad and cried (John 11:35). I know You understand how it feels to be sad. Help me see the best way to work through my sadness. **Jesus, thank You for understanding my feelings. Amen.**

Jesus,

The Bible says there is a time for sadness (Ecclesiastes 3:4). Thank You for letting me know that being sad sometimes is okay. It's normal. So today, Jesus, I bring my unhappy feelings to You. **Jesus, help me through my sad times. Amen.**

Hi Jesus,

Some days I'm sad because I've broken a toy or something important. Then I don't know how to fix it or make it better. That makes me sad. I'm trying to be more careful. **Jesus, would You help me learn to be more careful? Amen.**

Dear Jesus,

Things didn't turn out the way I wanted them to. That makes me sad. But the Bible says that everything works for the good of those who love You (Romans 8:28). I believe You and trust in You. **Thank You, Jesus, for making everything work out for my good—even if it doesn't seem like it right now. Amen.**

Dear Jesus,

We all lose people we love. We lose people who make us laugh and people who give the best hugs. Not having them around can make us sad. Jesus, I know You know how it feels to lose someone. I know You can help. **Please help me know the best way to say goodbye. Amen.**

Jesus,

In the Bible, You tell us that we are going to have trouble (John 16:33). Bad things are going to happen. But the best thing is, You also say that You have overcome the trouble in this world. **Jesus, thank You for being more powerful than even the biggest trouble. Amen.**

Jesus,

When other people are sad, it can make me sad. I know it makes You sad too. Help me see those people like You do. Jesus, teach me how to help others who are sad. **Help me to show Your love. Amen.**

Dear Jesus,

Sometimes I'm not very nice to myself. Sometimes I eat food that is bad for my body. Sometimes I don't want to rest like I should. And sometimes I say things that are not nice—about myself! Remind me that You love me and care for me. **Help me take care of my body and my mind. Amen.**

Dear Jesus,

When I'm sad or grumpy, I'm not always very nice. Instead of spreading joy, I make others feel bad. Jesus, help me to love others like You do. **Help me to be nice to everyone around me, even when I don't feel like being nice. Amen.**

Jesus,

When I'm sad, sometimes it feels like the bad feelings will never end. It seems like the rainclouds over my head will be there forever. Please remind me that's not true. **Help me, Jesus, to remember that the sadness will end. Amen.**

Jesus,

Thank You for my feelings—even the hard ones. Without sadness, my happiness wouldn't seem as happy. Without the bad, I wouldn't be as thankful for the good. **Even though I'm sad right now, Jesus, I'm thankful that You gave me my feelings. Amen.**

Dear Jesus,

You have given me so many people to cheer me up when I'm sad. They kiss my boo-boos. They wipe my tears. They pick me up when I fall. **Jesus, thank You for the people who cheer me up when I'm sad. Amen.**

Dear Jesus,

Being sad can sometimes feel like too much. Sometimes it can seem like no one understands. Sometimes it can seem like no one can fix it. But You can, Jesus. **Help me remember to talk to You when I'm sad. Amen.**

When I Am
AFRAID

"Be courageous! I have conquered the world."—Jesus

John 16:33

Jesus,

Thank You for Your power. When I am afraid, I can remember that You are bigger and stronger than any badness. **Thank You, Jesus, for being more powerful than anything in this world. Amen.**

Hi Jesus,

This is making me afraid today: _____. I just want to tell You about it. Thank You for caring about me and comforting me. **Thank You for always being there to listen to my fears. Amen.**

Wow, Jesus!

We can learn a whole lot about being brave from the people in the Bible. So many of them were brave and had courage because they trusted in You. Help us, Jesus, to learn about them. **Help me to remember the brave people in the Bible whenever I need to be brave too. Amen.**

Jesus,

Thank You for the example of Abraham in the Bible. He went wherever God told him to, even when he didn't know where he was going! He trusted and followed God just because God told him to. **Jesus, help me to follow God like Abraham did. Amen.**

Dear Jesus,

In the Bible, a tricky law said that Daniel could not pray to God (Daniel 6:6–9). But Daniel was brave and did what was right anyway. He kept praying to You. **Jesus, help me to do what's right even when it seems like everyone else is doing wrong. Amen.**

Jesus,

Esther was a brave queen of the Bible. She was willing to speak up when something was wrong. And God used her to save His people!

Jesus, help me to be brave like Esther and to speak up when something is wrong.

Amen.

Jesus,

When You met Your friends, Your disciples, they were so brave. You called them to follow You, and they stopped and dropped everything to go after You, even without knowing what would happen. **Jesus, help me to be brave and follow You too. Amen.**

Jesus,

You are the best example of being brave. When You faced really scary things, You prayed to Your Father, God. You asked God to do what He wanted to do with Your life, even if it would be scary. **Jesus, give me the courage to obey God even when I'm scared. Amen.**

Dear Jesus,

Sometimes our days can be scary, hard, or weird. But You promise to be with us always (Matthew 28:20). Help me to be strong and brave, Jesus. **Help me to find my strength and courage in You. Amen.**

Dear Jesus,

Sometimes I'm afraid of something that ends up being silly, like trying a new food. Sometimes I let my fear grow too big. And other times my fears are important. They keep me safe. Help me to know the difference. **Jesus, please calm my fears. Amen.**

Jesus,

Thank You for the people I can go to when I'm afraid. Thank You for the people who listen to my fears. Thank You for the people who hold me close and tell me that I'm safe. **Thank You, Jesus, for the people who help calm my fears. Amen.**

Jesus,

The Bible tells us to be strong and brave because God will be with us wherever we go (Joshua 1:9). I thank You that God's promises are true. **Jesus, help me to remember God's promises so that I can be strong and brave.**
Amen.

Jesus,

So many people work every day to keep me safe. There are firefighters and police officers. There are soldiers who are far away from their families. When I'm afraid, please help me remember all the people who are keeping me safe. **Jesus, please help those who keep me safe to be safe too. Amen.**

Dear Jesus,

When I'm afraid, I sometimes forget how much You have given me to keep me safe. I have a home where I can feel safe. I have a family who loves me. I have a warm bed with covers I can pull up tight. **Thank You for all the things that make me feel warm and safe. Amen.**

Jesus,

You've given me so many things
to help me when I'm scared.
Sometimes, my mommy or daddy
will hold me close. Or I'll squeeze one
of my pillows or stuffed animals as
tightly as I can. And when I do, I feel
a little better. **Thank
You, Jesus, for
cuddles to
make me
feel better.
Amen.**

Dear Jesus,

The Bible tells us that when Your friends, Your disciples, were on a boat in the middle of a stormy lake, they were scared and came to You for help. You calmed the storm—and their fears (Mark 4:35–41). **Jesus, please help me to remember that You are powerful enough to calm any storm—and my fears. Amen.**

Jesus,

When I'm afraid, sometimes I forget that You're right there with me. I forget about all the times that You've kept me safe. **When I'm afraid, Jesus, please help me to remember that You're watching over me. Amen.**

Dear Jesus,

Thank You for keeping me safe.
Thank You for calming my fears.
Thank You for reminding me to have
courage. Thank You for showing
me how to be brave. **Thank You,
Jesus, that with You, I am
always safe. Amen.**

When I Am
THANKFUL

"I praise you, Father, Lord of heaven and earth."—Jesus

Luke 10:21

Jesus,

Even You, the Son of God, took time to say thank You to God and praise Him for everything He created. Thank You, God, for the sun and moon and stars of heaven. And thank You, God, for the flowers and trees and fluffy animals. **Thank You, Jesus, for showing me how to be thankful. Amen.**

Hi Jesus,

Today I am thankful for

_____. I just wanted You to know! Thank You for the gifts I have today and every single day. **Help me, Jesus, to be thankful for all You give me every day. Amen.**

Wow, Jesus,

Thank You for all this yummy food!
From apples I can pick right off
the tree to an apple pie baked by
Mommy and me—You make all this
yummy food for us to taste and
eat. It gives my body energy, and it
makes me smile. **Thank You, Jesus
for yummy food. Amen.**

Jesus,

Thank You, thank You, for my home and everything in it! My family is so blessed to have a roof and walls and rooms where we can spend time together. Sometimes I forget that, Jesus. But today, I am so thankful. **Thank You, Jesus, for the gift of my home. Amen.**

Dear Jesus,

Thank You so much for the gift of my mommy. She takes care of our family and does so many helpful things that I don't even know about. Please give my mommy peace and rest. Help me remember to tell her how thankful I am for her. **Thank You, Jesus, for my mommy. Amen.**

Jesus,

Thank You for the daddy You've given me. He is smart and loving and teaches me so many things. Help me to learn from him and to be a good helper. Remind me to tell him how thankful I am to have him. **Thank You, Jesus, for my daddy. Amen.**

Dear Jesus,

Thank You for the special people I get to call family. From the youngest to the oldest, they all have something different to teach me and a different way that they love me. And I'm a special part of my family too! **Jesus, thank You for my family. Amen.**

Jesus,

Thank You for all the grown-ups who take the time to teach me things I need to know. Thank You for their patience and how they take their time with me. Because they care about me, they help me learn. I'm getting smarter every day! **Jesus, thank You for the grown-ups who teach me. Amen.**

Dear Jesus,

I am so thankful for our church, a place to worship You. Thank You for the songs we sing and the prayers we pray. Thank You for the people there who follow You with joy and show me how to join in too. **Thank You, Jesus, for my church. Amen.**

Oh, Jesus,

Thank You so much for the people who love me. They tie my shoes and fix my hair. They play with me and teach me and make me laugh and dry my tears and hug me tight. They show me that they love me every day, and I get to love them right back. **Jesus, thank You for wonderful people to love. Amen.**

Wow, Jesus,

Thank You for the sun! It makes it warm so that I can play outside. It shines its light after the rain to make a rainbow. It is just one of the many wonderful things You have created for us to enjoy. **Thank You, Jesus, for the sun and its light. Amen.**

Jesus,

Thank You for the singing birds. Their songs make me smile. I don't know how they find their food or how they carefully build their homes. But I know that if You take care of them, You will take care of me too (Matthew 6:26)! **Thank You, Jesus, for the birds. Amen.**

Dear Jesus,

Thank You for the clouds in the sky.
They help shade me from the sun.
They help bring rain. And sometimes
they even look like dogs and hearts
and hippos. But most of all, they
remind me of heaven, the place
where You are. **Thank You, Jesus,
for the clouds.
Amen.**

Hi Jesus,

Thank You for all the colors of the world. The bright red tulips, the green leaves on the trees, and the blue bluebird flying by—all the colors of the world are amazing to see. **Thank You for giving us such a beautiful world. Amen.**

Jesus,

Thank You for my five senses and all the ways I am able to hear and taste and see and touch and smell. I can explore the world because of my senses. And they help me learn and stay safe too. **Thank You for making my body able to see, hear, smell, touch, and taste so many wonderful things! Amen.**

Jesus,

Thank You for giving us work to do. Thank You for a chance to use my growing muscles. Thank You for the ways I can help around the house. Thank You for showing me that I can do hard things. **Thank You, Jesus, for work to do. Amen.**

Dear Jesus,

Thank You for rest. When my body is tired, rest recharges every part of me. When my mind is tired, rest helps it to think clearly again. Thank You for making rest an important part of my day and my week. **Thank You, Jesus, that I can rest. Amen.**

Jesus,

Thank You for the chance to learn. I can learn so much about You from the Bible. I can learn about the world around me in books and from other people. Thank You for giving me a big brain ready to learn lots and lots of things. **Thank You, Jesus, for all the things I can learn. Amen.**

Oh, Jesus,

Thank You so much for my friends! They make me laugh. They share their toys with me. They listen to what I have to say. And they are always ready to play. **Thank You, Jesus, for my friends. Amen.**

Dear Jesus,

Thank You for making so many beautiful people in this world. They have different colored eyes and hair and skin. They speak different languages and eat different foods and wear different clothes. And You love them all! **Thank You, Jesus, for people who show all the different kinds of beauty You have made. Amen.**

Dear Jesus,

Thank You for Your Word, the Bible. It's full of so many stories about You and Your people. But most of all, it's a book about how You love us. I want to spend my life learning about You. **Thank You, Jesus, for the Bible. Amen.**

Jesus,

Help me to be thankful no matter what. Even when I don't get exactly what I want. Even when I think I'm missing out. Even when I have everything I could wish for and so much more. **Help me to be thankful all the time, Jesus. Amen.**

When I
WORRY

"So don't worry, saying, 'What will we eat?' or 'What will we drink?' or 'What will we wear?'"—Jesus

Matthew 6:31

Jesus,

In the Bible, You say not to worry (Matthew 6:31). But I do. I worry about big things. I worry about little things. I worry about things I can't control. So help me, Jesus. **Help me not to worry. Amen.**

Dear Jesus,

Here is why I am worried today:
_____. But I know You already know how the day will turn out! You are in control. You make everything work out okay for the people who love You (Romans 8:28). **Jesus, help me to see how You are in control of everything. Amen.**

Jesus,

Sometimes I worry about my family and friends. I love them so much. I don't want anything bad to happen to them. But I know that You love them even more! **Jesus, take care of my friends and family today. Amen.**

Dear Jesus,

Sometimes I worry about messing things up. Help me to remember that I'm still learning and growing. I know I won't get it right all the time. **Help me to know, Jesus, that You love me no matter what. Amen.**

Jesus,

Thank You for all the reasons You tell us not to worry. The Bible shows how You care for everyone and everything You created, including the flowers and the smallest birds. **Whenever I start to worry, Jesus, help me to remember how much You care for me. Amen.**

Jesus,

In the Bible, Daniel prayed to God
no matter what. When Daniel was
punished for praying and locked in
a den of lions, he had big reasons
to worry! Still, God sent an angel
to keep him safe (Daniel 6:22). And
Daniel walked away from those lions
without a scratch! **Jesus, help me
to trust in You, even when I have
big reasons to worry. Amen.**

Jesus,

In the Bible, God reminded Jacob
that He would take care of him,
even when Jacob had to go far
from home. God said that He would
be with Jacob, watching over
him wherever he went (Genesis
28:15). You do the same for me!
Jesus, sometimes I worry. **Help
me remember that You are
watching over me,
wherever I go.
Amen.**

Jesus,

You remind us not to worry about what we will eat. You tell us that God feeds even the tiniest of birds in the trees. And God will certainly feed us too! **Jesus, thank You for reminding me that God feeds the birds, and God will feed me too. Amen.**

Dear Jesus,

You tell us not to worry about what we will wear. You say to remember the wildflowers. They don't sew clothes, yet they are still dressed more beautifully than a king (Matthew 6:26, 28–30). **Jesus, help me to remember that God takes care of the flowers. He will take care of me too. Amen.**

Jesus,

Thank You for the Bible. It's full of reminders of how God takes care of His people and His world. Anytime I'm worried, I can open the Bible and remember how much God loves us all. **Jesus, when I worry, help me remember all the ways God cares for me. Amen.**

Jesus,

Sometimes we think and worry about our future, about things that haven't happened yet. We think: What if tomorrow is a bad day? But You remind us not to worry about tomorrow. You remind us to think about today (Matthew 6:34). Today is a good day! **Jesus, help me not to worry about tomorrow. Amen.**

Dear Jesus,

The Bible reminds us of the best way to get rid of the worries: Your peace. It's a gift You give us every day (John 14:27). It's a gift we sometimes forget. **Jesus, help me always remember that You give peace. Amen.**

Dear Jesus,

Thank You for teaching me that worry doesn't help at all (Matthew 6:27). It doesn't make my day better. It doesn't make me brave. And it doesn't make me smile. **Jesus, help me to remember that worry doesn't help, but You do! Amen.**

Hi Jesus,

Even though worrying isn't helpful, I think we all worry sometimes. Even the people in the Bible who wrote beautiful songs to God had some big worries (Psalm 13:2). **Jesus, help me worry less by talking to You about it all. Amen.**

Dear Jesus,

Sometimes when I worry, I forget about all the people You've put around me to help me. So many times, they help calm my worry by explaining things to me. Thank You for the grown-ups You've put in my life. **Jesus, when I worry, remind me to tell the grown-ups who love me. Amen.**

Hi Jesus,

The Bible reminds us to talk to God instead of worrying! We can pray and tell Him about all our worries, all our thoughts, and all our needs (Philippians 4:6). **Thank You, Jesus, for always listening to everything I tell You. Amen.**

Jesus,

The Bible says that sleeping time
is a time for peace, not for worry
(Psalm 4:8). God watches over
me when I sleep, so I can dream
peacefully. **Thank You, Jesus, that
sleeping time is a peaceful time.
Amen.**

Jesus,

Worry just doesn't make sense.
When I start to worry, help me
remember all the reasons why
I shouldn't. I know You're bigger
than any worry, and You're always
watching over me. **When I start
to think about my worries,
Jesus, help me think about You
instead. Amen.**

When I Am
ANGRY

"For if you forgive others their offenses, your heavenly Father will forgive you as well."—Jesus

Matthew 6:14

Dear Jesus,

Sometimes I get angry when people hurt my feelings. But the Bible says that when we forgive others, God forgives us too. **Jesus, please help me forgive others when I am angry. Amen.**

Jesus,

Here's why I am angry today: _____. Help me understand why this made me angry. Can You help me know what to do with this feeling? **Jesus, show me a healthy way to deal with my anger. Amen.**

Dear Jesus,

Sometimes I get angry about things before I know the whole story. Sometimes I get mad before I know why something happened. There may be a good reason for the thing that happened. **Jesus, help me to stop and think and listen instead of getting angry. Amen.**

Jesus,

Sometimes when I get mad about how someone acted, I haven't thought about why they did what they did. Maybe my friend was angry. Maybe my sister was hurt or sad. I know You know the reason, Jesus. **Please help me be kind to people who are angry or hurting or sad. Amen.**

Jesus,

Sometimes I am selfish. I get angry because I want what someone else has. I know that's not the way I should act. I know I should share and be thankful for what I have. **Jesus, help me to remember how much I have and how blessed I am. Amen.**

Dear Jesus,

When I'm angry, I sometimes say or do things that hurt other people. I'm sorry. I don't want to yell or hit or say mean words. I want to stop and think about my words and actions before I hurt people. **Jesus, please help me to think of others, even when I am angry. Amen.**

Dear Jesus,

I know that God gave us our feelings. And anger is one of those feelings. But I know that feeling too much anger or being mad for too long can be bad for me. **Jesus, help me use my feelings in a way that's good for me and those around me. Amen.**

Jesus,

The Bible tells us that God is slow to get angry, and He is full of grace and love (Exodus 34:6). Help me to be more like Him so that I don't get mad easily. **Jesus, help me to be full of grace and love instead of anger. Amen.**

Jesus,

When I'm mad, I feel like I want to stay mad forever and ever. But the Bible tells me not to hold a grudge, not to stay angry for a long time (Leviticus 19:18). **Jesus, help me to let go of my anger quickly. Amen.**

Jesus,

The Bible says not to let the sun go down on my anger (Ephesians 4:26). I need to remember that it's not good to stay mad for a long time. And I especially shouldn't go to sleep while I'm still mad. **Jesus, help me to forgive so that I can go to bed with no anger in me. Amen.**

Dear Jesus,

When I am angry, I don't always want to talk to someone about it. But I know that people around me can help. **Jesus, help me remember to talk to a grown-up who can help me know what to do with my anger. Amen.**

Jesus,

Sometimes when I'm angry, I do mean things that I shouldn't. I use my hands and feet and body to show my anger and hurt other people. Please forgive me. **Help me, Jesus, to use my words to tell why I am angry. Amen.**

Dear Jesus,

Sometimes my anger is just because I have big feelings, and I don't know what to do with them. I may be tired or scared or hungry, but angry words come out. Help me to stop, take a deep breath, and use my brain to think. **Jesus, help me to think through my feelings and needs so that I can say better words. Amen.**

Jesus,

The Bible says that anger brings hurt and trouble (Psalm 37:8). Help me to be careful with my anger. I don't want to cause pain and trouble when I am angry. **Jesus, help me to use my feelings in a way that helps instead of hurts. Amen.**

Jesus,

The book of Proverbs in the Bible tells us that a fool gets angry easily (Proverbs 29:11). Jesus, I don't want to be foolish. I want to be wise. I want to be someone who is not easily angered. **Jesus, help me to be wise and slow, slow, slow to anger. Amen.**

Jesus,

The Bible says that anger is like a flood (Proverbs 27:4). I know how that feels. The feeling of hot anger flooding through me—it makes me feel out of control. **Jesus, please help me when I feel anger flooding my heart. Amen.**

Dear Jesus,

The Bible tells us that wise people turn away anger (Proverbs 29:8). When I feel anger coming, help me to turn my thoughts and think about something loving and calm instead. Show me how to do that, Jesus. **Please help me always to turn angry feelings into calm feelings. Amen.**

Dear Jesus,

When I am angry, help me to remember what the Bible says about anger. We should be slow to anger. Anger is harmful. And we shouldn't go to bed when we're still mad about something. **Jesus, most of all, when I am angry, help me to forgive, and help me to tell You all about my feelings. Amen.**

When I Feel
ALONE

"Remember, I am with you always."—Jesus

Matthew 28:20

Dear Jesus,

Thank You for telling us in the Bible that You are always with us. When I feel all alone, it helps to know that You are there, even if I can't see You. **Jesus, when I am lonely, help me to remember that You are with me. Amen.**

Hi Jesus,

Here's why I feel lonely today:
_____. I know that You
are listening. I know that You care.
And I know that You are with me.
**Jesus, thank You for listening
when I feel lonely. Amen.**

Dear Jesus,

When God created the world, He knew that we would need each other. He knew it wasn't good for us to be alone (Genesis 2:18), so He gave us families and friends and teachers and neighbors. **Jesus, thank You for the people God has given me so that I won't feel alone. Amen.**

Jesus,

The Bible tells us that Noah was alone in a different way. Even though lots of people were around, Noah was the only one listening to God (Genesis 7:1). In that way, Noah's loneliness was a good thing. He was alone because he did what was right. **Jesus, help me to obey You, even if I feel like I'm the only one doing it. Amen.**

Jesus,

In the Bible, Joshua was the new leader of God's people and had a big, hard job to do (Joshua 1). He must have felt so nervous and alone. But God was with him. And God told Joshua that He would not leave him alone. **Dear Jesus, when I feel lonely, remind me that God is with me, helping me do hard things. Amen.**

Dear Jesus,

In the Bible, God told His people that He would be with them, that He would help them and make them strong (Isaiah 41:10). Jesus, help me remember these words when I am tired or lonely. **Help me remember that God is with me, helping me and making me strong. Amen.**

Jesus,

When God's messenger, Elijah, felt alone, God was with him. God even sent an angel with bread for Elijah to eat and water for him to drink (1 Kings 19:6). God sent Elijah a helper too (19:21)! **Dear Jesus, help me remember that God cared for Elijah, and God cares for me when I feel alone. Amen.**

Oh, Jesus,

In the Bible, Job lost everything. He was so alone! When his friends came, they only made things worse (Book of Job). But God was with Job. God spoke to Job and made him feel better. He even gave him back what he had lost. **Jesus, help me to trust God to comfort me. Amen.**

Dear Jesus,

Sometimes when I feel lonely, I don't know why or what to say. In the Bible, one prayer just asks God to look our way, to see what we need, and to help us (Psalm 25:16). When I don't know how to ask for help, help me remember those words. **Jesus, look my way and help me. Amen.**

Jesus,

The Bible says that when we believe in You, we become family with everyone else who believes in You. We aren't strangers anymore. We are part of the family of God (Ephesians 2:19–22). When I feel alone, Jesus, help me to remember my great big family—people all over the world who love You and believe in You too! **Jesus, thank You for the family of God. Amen.**

Dear Jesus,

The Bible tells us that we are never alone when we feel sad and broken. God is close to us when our hearts are sad, when we need Him most (Psalm 34:18). **Jesus, help me to remember that I am never alone when I am sad. Amen.**

Dear Jesus,

I can look in the Bible to know exactly what to do when I am lonely. It says that when I come close to God, He will come close to me (James 4:8). Whenever I am lonely, I can simply talk to God, and He will be with me. **Jesus, thank You for helping me know what to do when I feel alone. Amen.**

Jesus,

The Bible tells us that God not only watches over His people, but He also sings over us (Zephaniah 3:17)! How can I ever feel lonely when I know that? **Jesus, whenever I feel lonely, help me to picture God right there, singing over me. Amen.**

Jesus,

When You were sad, You went away from the big groups of people so You could be alone (Matthew 14:13). You were alone on purpose! You showed us that being alone is good sometimes. It gives us time to think about our feelings. Maybe I need to do that too. **Jesus, thank You for showing me that being by myself is helpful sometimes. Amen.**

Dear Jesus,

Sometimes I forget one of the best cures for feeling lonely—a hug! So many people around me love me and would be happy to wrap me up in a big, warm hug. Thank You, Jesus, for those people. **Thank You, Jesus, for making hugs. Amen.**

Jesus,

Even when I am lonely, I know how much it helps to make someone else smile. Help me to always look for ways to help others. When I do, I know that it will make me happy too. **Jesus, help me to remember how good it feels to make someone else smile. Amen.**

Dear Jesus,

Sometimes, no matter what I do,
I just can't fix it when I feel lonely.
I don't always know what to do or
why I feel that way. But I know that
You have given me people to help.
**Jesus, when I am lonely, help me
to talk to a grown-up who loves
me. Amen.**

Jesus,

When I am lonely, I know I can always talk to You. I know You are always there, listening to me and loving me. I'm never really alone because You're right there, just a prayer away. **Thank You, Jesus, for always being there to talk to. Amen.**

When Someone Is
MEAN

"Pray for those who mistreat you."—Jesus

Luke 6:28

Jesus,

You tell us to pray for those who are mean to us (Luke 6:28). When someone is mean to me, I want to be mean back to them. I want to say things that aren't nice to them. But I know that You teach us better. **Jesus, help me to pray for those who are mean to me. Amen.**

Dear Jesus,

I need to tell You that _____ was mean to me this week. Their words and actions made me upset. Help them to see how they made me feel. Help me to be kind no matter what. **Jesus, please help me feel better. Amen.**

Jesus,

The Bible tells us that God hears the cries of those who are treated badly (Exodus 22:27). When someone is mean to me, it helps to know that God cares. He hears my cries. **Dear Jesus, help me to remember that even though someone is mean to me, God is listening. Amen.**

Jesus,

You teach that we are supposed to do good things to people who say mean things about us (Luke 6:28). Jesus, that is really, really hard to do. But You did it! I'm going to try to do it too. **Jesus, help me to be nice to those who say mean things to me.**
Amen.

Dear Jesus,

Thank You for showing us how to act toward someone who is mean to us. In the Bible, You teach us that when people are mean, we should talk to them about it first. If that doesn't work, we should talk to someone else, like a grown-up. **Jesus, when people are mean, help me act the way You tell me to. Amen.**

Jesus,

When someone is mean, sometimes the first thing I want to do is to be mean right back to them. But the Bible says not to do that (Proverbs 20:22). The Bible reminds us that God sees it all. He sees when people are mean. **Jesus, help me to trust that God will make things right again. Amen.**

Dear Jesus,

You say that we should treat others how we want to be treated (Matthew 7:12). That's hard to do sometimes, especially when people are mean. But help me, Jesus, to remember Your rule. **Help me to treat others the way I want them to treat me. Amen.**

Jesus,

The Bible teaches us to live in peace, to live without fighting or causing trouble with people around us (Romans 12:18). When we live in peace, the God of peace will be with us (2 Corinthians 13:11). Help me to do that, no matter what the people around me do. **Jesus, help me choose to live a peaceful life. Amen.**

Dear Jesus,

I know that people sometimes make bad choices. I know that even good people can say or do mean things. Jesus, help me to look past someone's mean words and actions and see that person the way You do—with love. **Jesus, help me to forgive people who are mean. Amen.**

Jesus,

So many Bible stories show us how to act when people are mean. Jesus, thank You for teaching us through stories and examples so that we can know how to act too. **Thank You for the Bible to show me what to do when someone is mean. Amen.**

Dear Jesus,

In the Bible story about Joseph, his brothers were so mean to him. But Joseph trusted that God would be with him. And God was! Joseph's brothers meant to hurt him, but God turned it around and used it to save a lot of people (Genesis 50:20). **Jesus, help me to remember that God is watching and working things out for my good. Amen.**

Jesus,

When You were alone in the desert, Satan tried to trick You. But You wouldn't let him. You knew God's Word. You knew that His Words were more powerful than any trick Satan tried to play (Matthew 4:4). **Dear Jesus, help me to remember God's words in the Bible when people try to trick me. Amen.**

Dear Jesus,

So many people were mean to You while You were here on earth. When the soldiers came to take You away, Your friend Peter took out his sword. But You told him to put it away (Matthew 26:52). You told Peter that those who hurt others will get hurt themselves. **Thank You, Jesus, for reminding me not to hurt others. Amen.**

Jesus,

When You were hurting, when people were being mean to You, You asked God to forgive them. You asked God to forgive them because they didn't know what they were doing (Luke 23:34). Jesus, help me to love people the way You do. **Help me to forgive people even when they hurt me. Amen.**

Dear Jesus,

Sometimes people are mean to other people because of their differences. They may look different. They may speak differently. They may have a different favorite food. But You made and love each of us! **Jesus, help me to see others the way You see them. Amen.**

Jesus,

You know better than anyone how mean this world can be. But You ask us to be different. The Bible reminds us that when the world is mean, we don't do as the world does. We do what God says (Romans 12:1–2). **Jesus, help me to be different and to act how God wants me to. Amen.**

Dear Jesus,

Sometimes when people say mean things, I want to say mean things too. But the Bible tells me that it's not good to use the same mouth to both praise God and say bad things about the people made in His image (James 3:9–10). **Jesus, help me to say only good things about the people God has made. Amen.**

Jesus,

You've taught us so much about how to treat people who are mean to us. You've taught us to pray for them, not to be mean back to them, and to act like God wants us to. **Jesus, help me to remember Your words and teachings when someone is mean to me. Amen.**

When I Need to
SHARE

"Give, and it will be given to you."—Jesus

Luke 6:38

Dear Jesus,

Sharing is hard. I know I'm supposed to. I know it's part of being a good friend. But sometimes I don't want to let others use what I have. Jesus, thank You for helping me. **Thank You for reminding me that I should give and share. Amen.**

Jesus,

I really should have shared today
when _____. I'm sorry. I'm
working on it. Help me to remember
Your words about being kind and
sharing what I have. **Jesus, forgive
me, and help me to remember
how important it is to share.
Amen.**

Jesus,

Sometimes I only share because I want someone to share with me. Or I want to hear someone tell me, "Good job!" But You tell us that we should share even if we won't get anything back (Luke 6:35). **Jesus, help me to share just because it's the right thing to do. Amen.**

Dear Jesus,

The Bible says that rich people should be happy to give to others (1 Timothy 6:17–18). But when I think about the wonderful things in my life, I realize that I might be a rich person too! So many people in the world are in need. **Jesus, help me to share and to give with a smile on my face. Amen.**

Hi Jesus,

The Bible tells us to work so that we will have something to share (Ephesians 4:28). Even though I'm too young to have a job, there's still work I can do. I can help pick up around the house so that my parents have more time. I can help make brownies for everyone to enjoy. **Jesus, show me ways that I can help and have something to share. Amen.**

Jesus,

The Bible says that God is pleased when we share (Hebrews 13:16). Even though it is hard to share sometimes, I want to do what pleases God. I want to do what He wants me to do. **Jesus, help me to remember that when I share, it makes God happy. Amen.**

Jesus,

You've taught that when we give, even more comes back to us (Luke 6:38). I know that's not the reason we should share. But it's nice to know that You see when we share. **Jesus, thank You for reminding me of how good it is to share. Amen.**

Dear Jesus,

Sometimes sharing isn't easy. I want to keep all my favorite things to myself. But the Bible says that being kind and sharing with my friends helps me too (Proverbs 11:17). When I am kind, I am blessed. **Jesus, help me always to be kind to others. Amen.**

Jesus,

You said that when we don't share with others, it's like we gave You nothing to eat when You were hungry (Matthew 25:42–45). When I don't share, I don't really think about how the other person feels. Or how it makes You feel. **Jesus, when I need to share, help me think about the feelings of others—especially Yours. Amen.**

Dear Jesus,

The Bible reminds us that when we give to people who need it, we are giving to God (Proverbs 19:17). Wow! I want to give to God since He has given me so much. **Jesus, help me to remember that sharing with others is giving to God. Amen.**

Dear Jesus,

The Bible tells us to share not only with the people who are nice to us but also with those who aren't nice to us (Romans 12:20). That's hard to do, Jesus, but I sure will try. **Jesus, help me remember to share with _everyone_. Amen.**

Jesus,

I know I'm supposed to think about the needs and feelings of others before I think of my own (Philippians 2:3). The Bible tells me so. And You show me how. But it's still really hard to do. Will You help me? **Jesus, please help me to think of others before I think of myself. Amen.**

Jesus,

The Bible talks about giving to others as being "refreshed" (Proverbs 11:25 NIV). It's like getting a cold glass of lemonade on a sunny day. Help me to remember this word picture when I need to share. **Jesus, help me to remember that sharing will make me feel refreshed. Amen.**

Dear Jesus,

Your friend John the Baptist said sharing looked like this: someone who had two shirts gave to the person who had no shirt (Luke 3:11). Jesus, I have two shirts. I have two toys. I have two snacks. **Please, Jesus, help me to see those who have none so that I can share with them. Amen.**

Jesus,

I have so much that I could share, and I'm not really sure of the best way to do it. But I know my parents and other grown-ups can help me. **Jesus, show me the best way to share my things and help someone who needs them. Amen.**

Dear Jesus,

The Bible tells us that we will put all our love and care into the things we treasure most (Luke 12:34). Jesus, I don't want my toys, my food, or any of my stuff to be the things I care about most. I want to love You and the people in my life the most. **Jesus, help me to think carefully about the things I treasure most. Amen.**

Jesus,

The Bible reminds us to love with our actions, not just with our words (1 John 3:18). You are the best example of showing Your love through the things You did. Jesus, help me to learn from Your example. **Help me to love people with the things I do each and every day. Amen.**

Dear Jesus,

Thank You for teaching me how to share with others. Thank You for showing me with Your life how to put others first. Jesus, help me to follow Your example every day. **Jesus, help me to share with others the way You want me to. Amen.**

When I Need
HELP

"Ask, and it will be given to you."—Jesus

Matthew 7:7

Dear Jesus,

You are so good to us. You tell us that if we ask, it will be given to us (Matthew 7:7). But You also know what is best for us. You know how to give us what we need, even if it's different from what we think we need. **Jesus, thank You for knowing the best way to help me. Amen.**

Hi Jesus,

I needed help today when

_____. Help me always to
ask for help when I need it. Help me
to remember that I have people all
around me who love me and want
to help. **Jesus, the family and
friends and teachers who help
me are gifts. Thank You! Amen.**

Jesus,

I have to ask for help all the time. I know I'm little. But I want to do things all by myself. Please help me to remember that it's okay to ask for help. Please help me to remember that I'm growing. **Jesus, please help me to be patient with myself. Amen.**

Jesus,

This world sometimes feels big and new, and sometimes I just don't understand things. I need help. I know that You have put smart people here to love me and help me. I know that I have a lot to learn. **Please help me to stop and ask for help when I don't understand. Amen.**

Dear Jesus,

I love to give things like presents and hugs to the people I love! But You said that God knows how to give even better gifts than I do (Matthew 7:11). Help me to remember that God loves giving and helping. **Jesus, when I need help, please help me remember to ask God. Amen.**

Jesus,

The Bible tells about a time Moses was doing too much work. A wise man asked Moses why he was doing it all alone. He told Moses to ask for help (Exodus 18:18). Jesus, help me to remember that I don't have to do it all alone. **Help me to ask for help instead of trying to do it all by myself. Amen.**

Jesus,

The Bible says we should carry each other's burdens, which means helping other people through hard things (Galatians 6:2). Everyone needs help sometimes. Jesus, help me to remember that it is always okay to ask for help. **Thank You, Jesus, for giving us each other to help us make it through hard things. Amen.**

Oh, Jesus,

The Bible tells a story about a young king who got advice from wise people. But this young king didn't listen, and it didn't go well for him (1 Kings 12). Jesus, please help me to ask for advice when I need it. **Most of all, Jesus, when I ask for help, please help me to listen. Amen.**

Hi Jesus,

Sometimes I get tired of waiting. Sometimes I want help right now. Sometimes I don't want to wait to be able to do something. But the Bible says that people who wait patiently for God are happy (Isaiah 30:18). That is so hard to do. **Jesus, help me to wait patiently when I need help. Amen.**

Dear Jesus,

Thank You for Your reminder of where our help comes from. Our help comes from God, who made heaven and the whole wide world (Psalm 121:2). If God is powerful enough to create and give life to everything and anything, then He can help me too! **Jesus, thank You for reminding me that my help comes from God. Amen.**

Dear Jesus,

I can list so many people who help me, like my parents, grandparents, and teachers. The Bible says that it is good to have the help and advice of many people (Proverbs 11:14). Thank You for all the wise people around me. **Please help me to remember that it's good to go to them, and to You, when I need help. Amen.**

Jesus,

Sometimes I feel silly asking for help when I don't know what to do. But the Bible reminds me that it's good to listen to advice (Proverbs 12:15). Jesus, help me to remember this. **Help me to remember that it's never silly to ask for help. Amen.**

Dear Jesus,

The Bible tells us about a big, strong soldier who asked You for help (Matthew 8:5). Of course You helped him! If even a strong soldier can ask You for help, I can too. **Jesus, help me never to feel too big or strong to ask You for help. Amen.**

Jesus,

The Bible talks about being too proud to ask for help (Proverbs 11:2). I know what that feels like. I like to do things by myself! But I also know that I can learn a lot when I tell others that I need help. **Jesus, help me never be too proud to ask for help. Amen.**

Dear Jesus,

It's easy to ask You for help. The Bible says that anytime we ask, You will hear us (1 John 5:14). Thank You, Jesus, for this reminder. **Thank You for listening any and every time I ask for help. Amen.**

Jesus,

I know that You created us to be good at different things. I know I'm not good at some things yet, and I may need help. But I'm really good at other things, like _____, and I can help my friends and family with those things! Thank You for our different gifts. **Jesus, help me to use my gifts to help others. Amen.**

Dear Jesus,

No matter what I need help with, I know You can help. The Bible reminds us that we can do all things with You, because You give us our strength (Philippians 4:13). **Whatever I need, whenever I need help, Jesus, help me remember to come to You. Amen.**

Jesus,

Thank You for being there when I need help with the big things and the little things. Thank You for telling us just to ask. You will give. As I grow, I know I will need a lot of help. **More than anything, Jesus, help me grow to be more like You each day. Amen.**

When I Need to
FORGIVE

"Forgive, and you will be forgiven."—Jesus

Luke 6:37

Dear Jesus,

In the Bible, You tell us simply to forgive. But to forgive, I have to decide not to be mad or grumpy at someone because they did something wrong. Still, because You said it, I know it's important. When I need to forgive, help me to focus on Your words instead of my feelings. **Thank You, Jesus, for reminding me to forgive. Amen.**

Dear Jesus,

Today I need to forgive
_____. Can
You help me understand why that
person acted that way? Help me to
remember that other people's words
and actions may come from their
own hurting. **Jesus, help me to
forgive them. Amen.**

Dear Jesus,

I know that God is always watching over us. You remind us that He sees the way we forgive (Matthew 6:14–15). I want to treat others the way God wants me to. And I want to forgive the way God wants me to. **Jesus, help me to remember that God cares about how I forgive others. Amen.**

Dear Jesus,

When Joseph's brothers treated him really badly, his father told him to forgive (Genesis 50:17). Joseph's father reminded him that forgiveness is important, and Joseph listened. **Jesus, help me to listen and learn when others teach me how to forgive. Amen.**

Dear Jesus,

I know how important it is to be kind to everybody, all the time. And the Bible tells me that forgiveness is part of being kind (Ephesians 4:32). **Jesus, help me to be kind, and help me to forgive. Amen.**

Dear Jesus,

The Bible says that if I believe in You, that if I belong to You, I will show it. I will be patient and gentle and caring with others. When I'm upset with people for something they did, I will forgive (Colossians 3:12–13). Help me to act like I belong to You, Jesus. **Help me to be patient, gentle, and forgiving. Amen.**

Dear Jesus,

When I find it hard to forgive, it helps to remember that I need forgiveness too. I mess up all the time, and I would be so sad if I weren't forgiven for the things I do wrong. **Jesus, help me to remember that everyone needs forgiveness, including me! Amen.**

Dear Jesus,

In the Bible, Peter asked You how many times he had to forgive someone. You told him that he should forgive not just seven times but "seventy times seven" (Matthew 18:22). I don't know how many that is, but it sounds like a lot! **Jesus, please help me to forgive again and again, as many times as You want me to. Amen.**

Dear Jesus,

You say that forgiving others is something we should do all the time. Every time we pray, and before we pray, we should forgive anyone we need to (Mark 11:25). Who do I need to forgive today? Help me to remember. **Jesus, help me to forgive others every time I pray. Amen.**

Dear Jesus,

You showed us how to love better than anyone on earth. The Bible says that love helps us to forgive the unkind things that people do and say (Proverbs 10:12). Help me to love others like You do. **Jesus, when someone I love says something unkind, help me to forgive. Amen.**

Dear Jesus,

The Bible tells us something special about forgiveness. It says that good things happen when we forgive. When we forgive, love grows (Proverbs 17:9). **Jesus, help me to sprinkle lots of forgiveness so that love grows everywhere I go. Amen.**

Jesus,

We are supposed to forgive the way God has forgiven us (Ephesians 4:32). But sometimes I'm not sure what that looks like. **Jesus, show me all the ways God has forgiven me so that I can forgive that way too. Amen.**

Oh, Jesus,

The Bible says that when God forgives us, He takes away our sins "as far as the east is from the west" (Psalm 103:12). I don't know how far that is, but it sounds like a long, long way away. **Jesus, help me to forgive as far as the east is from the west. Amen.**

Jesus,

God knows everything. But when He forgives us, He forgets all our sins (Hebrews 10:17). I don't know how that's possible, but that's how much He loves us. **Jesus, help me to forgive and forget like God does. Amen.**

Dear Jesus,

The Bible tells us a lot about forgiveness. But when it's time for me to forgive, sometimes it's hard to understand *how* I should forgive. What do I say? What do I do? **Jesus, help me to know how to show someone I forgive them. Amen.**

Jesus,

Sometimes, I really have a hard time forgiving others when they hurt my feelings or make me angry. I know I should choose to forgive anyway. I know that I should forgive others the way that You forgive me. **Help me, Jesus, to choose to forgive like You do. Amen.**

Jesus,

Sometimes I don't understand why people do the things they do. And that's okay. I don't have to. You know. And You understand. And You still ask me to forgive. **Jesus, help me to forgive even when I don't understand. Amen.**

Dear Jesus,

Forgiveness makes us feel better. Forgiveness makes others feel better. But most importantly, forgiveness makes us more like You. **Jesus, help me to remember that the biggest reason to forgive is to make me more like You. Amen.**

When I Need

PEACE

"My peace I give to you."—Jesus
John 14:27

Oh, Jesus,

You've given us the best gift! You give us Your peace. Your peace calms the storms. It cleans up the messes. It makes our hearts feel better when they are sad. **Thank You, Jesus, for giving me Your peace. Amen.**

Dear Jesus,

Today I need peace and calm because _____.
Help me to see this hard thing the way that You would. Help me to feel the peace that only You can give. **Help me, Jesus, to find peace today. Amen.**

Dear Jesus,

Thank You for giving us peace. Help me remember that Your peace is different from any other peace in this world. It's more than a quiet room. It's more than a smooth, still lake. It is a calm that I feel in my heart and mind and soul. **Jesus, let me have the peace that only You can give. Amen.**

Oh, Jesus,

I am sad and hurting, and I don't
know what to do. But the Bible says
that You are bigger than all the
hurting in this world (John 16:33).
When I am facing something big,
help me to close my eyes and see
You there, too, the One who is bigger
than all the bad in the world. **Jesus,
thank You for standing with me.
Amen.**

Dear Jesus,

When I need peace, when I am nervous or afraid, help me to remember You. Your Word says that You keep me safe (Psalm 121:7). **Thank You, Jesus, for loving me and caring for me and keeping me safe. Amen.**

Jesus,

Sometimes I feel so small, so weak. Sometimes my brain is all jumbled up. And then Your Word reminds me that God gives me strength (Psalm 29:11). He gives me peace. And that is all I need. **Thank You, Jesus, that I can be strong and I can be peaceful, all because of You. Amen.**

Jesus,

I've never thought about *looking* for peace. But that's just what the Bible says to do (Psalm 34:14). Where do I find it? How can I see it? I'm not sure, but I do know that You will help me find it. **Jesus, please help me as I look for peace. Amen.**

Jesus,

If my family is super busy or someone is in a bad mood, *nothing* feels peaceful. But Your Word says that those who love to learn from You will have lots of peace (Psalm 119:165). When my family learns from You and does what You say, our minds and hearts and home are at peace. **Thank You, Jesus, for teaching me how to live at peace. Amen.**

Dear Jesus,

Long, long ago when Your people needed peace, they would cry out to You (Psalm 120:1). That means they would talk to You and ask You for help. Your Word says that when we cry out to You, You answer. **Dear Jesus, thank You for listening when I cry out to You. Amen.**

Dear Jesus,

I want to have peace. And I want to be someone who helps other people feel peaceful too. Your Word says that when we spread and share peace, we will have joy (Proverbs 12:20). **Jesus, help me to be someone who spreads peace. Amen.**

Jesus,

The Bible says that there's a time for everything, even peace (Ecclesiastes 3:8). I know that every day won't be calm and peaceful. **Jesus, be with me all the time, on days with peace and on days without peace. Amen.**

Jesus,

When I need peace, I know exactly where to go—to You! The Bible says that You are the Prince of Peace (Isaiah 9:6). So when I am feeling angry or confused or scared, I will come straight to You. **Jesus, thank You for being the Prince of Peace. Amen.**

Dear Jesus,

The Bible says that when we trust in God, we are in *perfect* peace (Isaiah 26:3). I know I can't be perfect, and that's okay. But You are perfect, and You share Your perfect peace with me. **Jesus, help me to trust in God so that I can have perfect peace. Amen.**

Dear Jesus,

The Bible tells us that God will make peace for His people (Isaiah 26:12). He made the whole world, and He made peace too! **Jesus, when I feel scared or worried, remind me that God is the Maker of peace. Amen.**

Jesus,

Sometimes the way I act can make my day calm or crazy. Sometimes the way others act can make my day calm or crazy too. But the Bible says that making the right choices will bring peace (Isaiah 32:17). **Jesus, help me make good choices to fill my day with peace. Amen.**

Dear Jesus,

Sometimes we lose our peace because we forget who's watching over us. We forget who is in control. But the Bible reminds us to be still and to remember that God is God. He is in control, watching over us (Psalm 46:10). **Jesus, no matter what happens, help me to be still and to remember who is in control. Amen.**

Oh, Jesus,

So many people in this world need peace. They might be scared or lonely or hungry. For some of them, only You know the problem. Please be with them right now. **Jesus, please help people all over the world who need Your peace. Amen.**

Jesus,

I know that life will not always be peaceful. I know that I will have times when I am sad or angry or scared or confused. When I feel that way, help me always to remember the best place to go is You! **Jesus, help me to come straight to You when I need peace. Amen.**

When I've Done Something WRONG

"Pray like this: . . . Forgive the sins we have done."—Jesus

Matthew 6:9, 12 ICB

Dear Jesus,

I know that You care about me. And I know that You know everything about me—You even know all the times I sin and do things that are wrong. **Thank You for knowing me so well and loving me even when I mess up. Amen.**

Dear Jesus,

I've done something wrong
today. Here's what I've done:
_____. Please forgive
me, Jesus. Please help me do the
right thing next time. **Jesus, thank
You for forgiving me for what
I've done wrong. Amen.**

Jesus,

The Bible is full of stories about God's people. Some of those stories are about people who did wrong and how God forgave them. I want to learn more about You and Your people. I want to learn more about right and wrong and God's big love. **Jesus, thank You for the Bible that teaches me so much. Amen.**

Jesus,

In the Bible, when Adam and Eve disobeyed God, they were afraid and tried to hide (Genesis 3). When I do something wrong, I want to run and hide too! God still found Adam and Eve. After He asked what had happened, they told Him what they had done wrong. **Jesus, help me to be honest and tell the truth when I've done something wrong. Amen.**

Jesus,

In the Bible, God asked Jonah to do something, but Jonah didn't just disobey—he ran the other way! After spending three nights praying in the belly of a fish, Jonah went to do exactly what God had asked him to do (Jonah 1–3). **Jesus, help me always to obey the first time! Amen.**

Dear Jesus,

In the Bible, as Moses was leading God's people to the Promised Land, they whined and complained and disobeyed. Bad things happened because of their bad choices. But God still fed them and led them and loved them well. **Jesus, thank You for loving me even when I make bad choices. Amen.**

Dear Jesus,

When I do something wrong, I feel icky and guilty inside. But the Bible says that God cares about us even when we disobey Him, and He will forgive us when we ask (Daniel 9:9). Will You remind me of God's care the next time I mess up and feel bad? **Jesus, please help me quickly tell You and ask for forgiveness when I disobey. Amen.**

Jesus,

In the Bible, when King David did
something really bad, God sent
a man named Nathan to show
him what he'd done wrong. David
was sorry, and God forgave him
(2 Samuel 12). Friends and family
like Nathan are important! **Jesus,
thank You for people who love
me and show me when I've done
wrong. Amen.**

Jesus,

When I do something wrong, I get in trouble with my parents or teachers. I have to clean up the mess I made. Or I have to say I'm sorry. Sometimes I have something fun taken away from me. The Bible says that when God disciplines us, it's because He loves us (Hebrews 12:6). I know it's the same for grown-ups too. **Jesus, thank You for grown-ups who love me enough to teach me what is right and wrong. Amen.**

Jesus,

When someone does something wrong to me, it can make me so mad. I want to do the same thing back to them. But the Bible says not to do something wrong just because someone was not nice to me (Romans 12:17). **Jesus, help me remember *not* to do wrong even if someone else did. Amen.**

Dear Jesus,

Sometimes when my friends are breaking the rules, I want to break the rules too. But I know this isn't right. The Bible says that being around people who make bad choices every day can teach me to make bad choices too (1 Corinthians 15:33). **Jesus, help me choose good friends who make good choices. Amen.**

Jesus,

Sometimes I know what I'm about
to do is wrong, but I do it anyway.
When I want to do something
wrong, help me to remember that
You taught me how to pray for
help. You showed me how to ask
not to be tempted to do bad things
(Matthew 6:13). **Jesus, help me
remember Your words when I
have to choose between right
and wrong. Amen.**

Jesus,

You've taught us to treat others the way we want to be treated (Matthew 7:12). Sometimes, I don't do that at all! I treat others in ways that I'd *never* want to be treated. I'm sorry! Help me to do better. **Jesus, help me treat others the way I want to be treated. Amen.**

Dear Jesus,

The Bible tells us that when we have Your words in our heart, they help us choose right over wrong (Psalm 119:11). Jesus, help me to listen to and know the words You've given us. **Jesus, help me to keep Your words in my heart so that I do the right thing. Amen.**

Dear Jesus,

The Bible tells us to obey our parents, because it's the right thing to do (Ephesians 6:1). I know this. But sometimes, it is so hard to do. Jesus, help me to listen, to really listen to my parents and the grown-ups who love me. **Jesus, help me obey my parents and do what is right. Amen.**

Jesus,

Sometimes I'm not sure what is right and what is wrong. A friend might say it's okay for me to break a rule or to be mean to somebody. Sometimes I get confused and don't know which way to go. But the Bible says that God decides what is right or wrong (Micah 6:8). **Jesus, when I wonder what is right or wrong, help me remember to talk to God first and follow Him! Amen.**

Jesus,

Sometimes I feel so silly for making the wrong choice. But the Bible tells us that You understand when we are weak. You understand when we're tempted because You were tempted too (Hebrews 4:15). But You never sinned, and You never messed up. **Jesus, thank You for Your example of always choosing the right thing. Amen.**

Jesus,

I'm not perfect. You know that. And
no matter how hard I try, I am going
to mess up. I'm going to make wrong
choices. Help me to keep learning
the Bible so that I can make right
choices. But more importantly,
**Jesus, help me to come to
You and ask for forgiveness
when I do
something
wrong.
Amen.**

When I Don't Know
WHAT TO DO

"Not my will, but yours, be done."—Jesus

Luke 22:42

Dear Jesus,

When I don't know what to do, I can always look to You. When You were struggling with doing something hard, You prayed to Your Father, God. You said You would do what He wanted, not what You wanted. **Jesus, help me to be like You and to look for what God wants, not what I want. Amen.**

Jesus,

Today, I don't know what to do about

_____. Help me, Jesus.

Show me what You would do. Help

me know what God wants me to do.

And, until I know, Jesus, help me to

wait. **Jesus, please help me when

I don't know

what to do.

Amen.**

Dear Jesus,

The Bible says I can always ask God for what I need. And when I don't know what to do, I can just talk to God about it! I know that He is listening and that He cares. **Jesus, thank You for listening when I ask You for help. Amen.**

Jesus,

Sometimes, the world is big and scary. I don't always know what to do or how to be brave. But the Bible says that God is my strength, even when the world around me seems scary or confusing (Psalm 46:1). **Jesus, help me to remember that God is my strength. Amen.**

Jesus,

I know that You are listening. That makes me feel so safe and loved! The Bible says that when I'm unsure or worried or scared to do something, God can make me feel loved. He brings me happiness (Psalm 94:19)! **Jesus, thank You for helping me feel safe and happy. Amen.**

Dear Jesus,

When I don't know what to do, sometimes I ask everyone but God. I know that is so silly, but sometimes I just forget. The Bible says that God is the One who helps us (Isaiah 41:13). **Jesus, when I don't know what to do, remind me to go to God, the One who can always help me. Amen.**

Jesus,

Sometimes making a tough choice makes me feel so helpless, so confused. But the Bible tells me that God didn't make me to feel that way. God gives me power. He gives me love. And He gives me self-control (2 Timothy 1:7). **Jesus, help me to use the gifts God has given me to know the best things to do each day. Amen.**

Oh, Jesus,

You have given me so many people who love me, people like

_____. Because of You, they are all here to help me. The Bible says that when many people help us and give us advice, our plans will work (Proverbs 15:22). **Jesus, thank You for the people You've put here to help me. Amen.**

Jesus,

I have so many questions. What will I be when I grow up? What will I wear *tomorrow*? What am I having for lunch *today*? But one answer is easy: Who should I think about first each day? God (Matthew 6:33)! When I think about God first, all those other answers are a lot easier to figure out too. **Jesus, help me to think about God first every day—and to let Him take care of the rest. Amen.**

Dear Jesus,

When we don't know what to do, we can follow Your two-step plan: "Believe in God; believe also in me" (John 14:1). Even though that sounds easy, it's really enough! When I believe in Your power and goodness, I can have Your peace. **Jesus, when I don't know what to do, remind me to just believe in You. Amen.**

Jesus,

In the Bible, when God's people didn't know what to do, Moses told them, "Don't do anything." He told them that they only needed to be still, because God would fight for them (Exodus 14:14). **Jesus, help me to remember that sometimes I just need to be still and let God work. Amen.**

Dear Jesus,

In the Bible, when Esther was faced with a tough decision, she trusted God to help. When her people were in danger, she trusted God to take care of her. And in the end, they were saved. **Jesus, when I don't know what to do, help me to trust You. Amen.**

Jesus,

You remind us that when we need something, we just need to ask You, look for You, and knock on Your door (Luke 11:9). I know You're talking about asking You for what we need. But I like to picture a real door, where I knock, and You open it all the way and smile. **Jesus, thank You for always answering when I knock on Your door. Amen.**

Oh, Jesus,

Sometimes I forget. I forget how big You are, how smart You are, and how much You love me. I forget that You don't think about things the same way I do (Isaiah 55:8). And when I'm upset and don't know what to do, I forget that You already know. You know how I'm feeling, and You know what I should do. **Jesus, I'm so thankful that You have it all figured out. Amen.**

Dear Jesus,

The Bible reminds me to wait patiently for the Lord (Psalm 37:7). This sounds easy. But waiting isn't easy. And waiting *patiently* is even harder. But because Your Word tells me to, I will try. **Jesus, when I don't know what to do, help me to wait patiently for You. Amen.**

Jesus,

The Bible says that You are good to those who learn to look and wait for You (Lamentations 3:25). So there's no need to ever wonder what to do—I just need to look for You, talk to You, listen to You, and learn from You. **Thank You, Jesus, for being all the answers I ever need. Amen.**

Dear Jesus,

In the Bible, when God's people were sad and worried and wondered what to do, God reminded them of His plans. He already had plans for their future—good plans, plans that were full of hope (Jeremiah 29:11). You took care of them, and You'll do the same for me. **Jesus, thank You for having good plans for me! Amen.**

Dear Jesus,

You are such a good listener. No matter how big or small my problem is, You are there, You are listening, and You can help. Jesus, when I don't know what to do, I will always come to You. **Thank You for always listening to me. Amen.**

When I Have to Do

HARD
THINGS

*"All things are
possible with God."*—Jesus

Mark 10:27

Dear Jesus,

I have to do a lot of hard things in a lot of different ways. It may be hard for my brain, like learning to count really high. It may be hard for my feelings, like losing a friend. Or it may just be hard to finish, like cleaning my room. **Thank You, Jesus, for being with me while I do hard things. Amen.**

Hi Jesus,

This is a hard thing I have to do
soon: _____.
I'm not looking forward to it. I know
I'm going to have to be strong. But I
know I can do it. I know You are with
me. **Jesus, please help me to do
this hard thing. Amen.**

293

Jesus,

Sometimes I forget why I need to do hard things. I think so much about how hard it will be that I forget how much better it will be once I've done it. I know I'll feel better after I say "I'm sorry" when I've messed up or after I go to the doctor when I'm sick. **Jesus, help me to think about the good that happens when I do hard things. Amen.**

Dear Jesus,

So many people in the Bible did hard things. And in their stories, God helped them. When I am having a hard time, help me remember these Bible stories. **Jesus, thank You for telling us about people who did hard things—and the God who helped them. Amen.**

Jesus,

The Bible says Joshua was trying to lead God's people into a city, but there was a big, rock wall in the way (Joshua 6)! God told them to march around the city, and the wall would fall down. As silly as it sounds, it worked! **Jesus, help me to remember that sometimes God does the hard work if we just obey Him! Amen.**

Oh, Jesus,

I don't know that I could face a giant like David did in the Bible (1 Samuel 17). But David stood up to that giant because he knew God was with Him. And even though David was much smaller than the giant, he knew God was bigger. He was right! **Jesus, when I have to do hard things, help me to have a faith as big as David's. Amen.**

Jesus,

In the Bible, Daniel prayed to God even when he knew bad things would happen because of it. Jesus, sometimes it's hard to pray to You when no one else is. It's hard to tell others about You when they don't know who You are. **Jesus, help me to be brave like Daniel and to talk to You—and about You—no matter what. Amen.**

Oh, Jesus,

You did the hardest thing of all. You left heaven to be with us. Then You gave up Your life so that we could be forgiven. I can't imagine doing anything that hard. But I don't have to because You did it for me. **Thank You, Jesus, for doing the hardest thing of all. Amen.**

Jesus,

Your friends, the disciples, showed us how to do hard things. After You went back to heaven, they went into the world to tell everyone about You. But not everyone wanted to hear. Still, the disciples kept doing what You had asked them to do, telling the world about You. **Jesus, help me to tell the world about You, even when it's hard. Amen.**

Dear Jesus,

When I'm doing hard things,
sometimes I want to stop and give
up. But You knew that we would
face hard things. And when You were
on earth, You taught the people
to pray and not give up (Luke 18:1).
**Jesus, when things are hard,
help me remember
to pray and not
give up. Amen.**

Jesus,

The Bible says that God will hold us up with His right hand (Isaiah 41:10). I love thinking about that! When I feel tired or scared or want to give up, I will think about God's big, strong hand holding me. **Jesus, help me always to remember God holding me up. Amen.**

Dear Jesus,

When God's people were slaves in Egypt, they had to do some very hard things. God made a way for them to get through them all. He even split a sea in two! Then the people sang, "The LORD is my strength and my song" (Exodus 15:2). God made them strong—and happy too! **Jesus, help me to remember this—that God is my strength and my happy song. Amen.**

Oh, Jesus,

Sometimes I feel so small, so weak. But You tell me in the Bible that all I need is You! You are powerful, and Your power works best through my weaknesses (2 Corinthians 12:9). **Thank You, Jesus, that when I am weak, Your power is strong. Amen.**

Dear Jesus,

It's hard to choose the right thing sometimes. But the Bible says that God is faithful and always there for me. It says that You will give me strength and protect me (2 Thessalonians 3:3). **Thank You, Jesus, for protecting me every day. Amen.**

Dear Jesus,

I love hearing what the Bible says about God's power. He is amazing! When I have to do hard things, I need *all* these reminders. God gives power and strength to us when we're weak (Isaiah 40:29). **Jesus, when I'm out of power, help me to remember God's mighty power. Amen.**

Jesus,

I like to run, but running a race is hard! It takes all my muscles and all my mind to win a race. The Bible tells us that life is kind of like running a race. And we should do our best, as if we were running to win a prize (1 Corinthians 9:24)! **Jesus, help me to stay strong and keep my focus on You while I'm running through this life! Amen.**

Jesus,

Thank You for helping me when I need to do something hard. When I see friends having trouble doing hard things, I know how to help! I can tell them how You make us brave and help us do hard things. **Jesus, help me tell my friends how You can make them brave. Amen.**

Dear Jesus,

Thank You for all Your reminders that I can do hard things. No matter what comes my way, I can do them all with You by my side. You make everything possible! **Jesus, help me remember that You are always with me. Amen.**

When I Don't
UNDERSTAND

"Don't let your hearts be troubled."—Jesus

John 14:1

Dear Jesus,

You already knew there would be things I don't understand. That's why You said, "Don't let it bother you. Just believe" (John 14:1). When I believe in You and Your wisdom and love, I understand everything I need to know. **Thank You, Jesus, for understanding everything so that I don't have to. Amen.**

Jesus,

Here's something I don't understand:
_____. Maybe I need
to learn more about it. Maybe
I just need to let You take care
of it. **Jesus, help me to have
Your peace about this thing
that I don't
understand.
Amen.**

Jesus,

There are a billion things we don't know about the world. The Bible talks about some of those things, like the path of the wind or how bones are formed (Ecclesiastes 11:5), and on and on and on. When I think about all the things I don't know, I realize just how much God *does* know. **Thank You, Jesus, for reminding me of the God who knows everything. Amen.**

Oh, Jesus,

God knows anything and everything. The Bible shows us that what we know could never, *ever* compare with how much God knows. God decided how big the earth would be. He told the morning when to start. He has walked in the deepest parts of the ocean (Job 38). He knows *ev-er-y-thing*. **Thank You, Jesus, that I can know the One who knows everything. Amen.**

Dear Jesus,

I'm still little, so there's a whole lot that I don't understand. But the Bible reminds me that God is God (Isaiah 41:10). I don't need to understand everything—because God does! On days when I don't understand anything else, help me to at least understand *that*. **Jesus, help me always remember that God is my God. Amen.**

Jesus,

Even when we think we *do* understand something, the Bible tells us not to depend on ourselves (Proverbs 3:5–6). It's not that we *shouldn't* learn and understand things, but that we should trust God more. **Jesus, help me trust God more than the things I learn and understand. Amen.**

Dear Jesus,

The Bible tells us how to understand what God says is good and pleasing (Romans 12:2). Whatever I'm told, whatever I learn, I can ask, "What does God say about this?" When I do, I will begin to learn about the things God loves. **Jesus, help me learn about the things that are good and pleasing to God. Amen.**

Jesus,

No matter what I think I understand, God understands more. No matter what I have planned, God's plans are bigger and better. And the Bible tells me that God's plans will win (Proverbs 19:21). **Jesus, I am so thankful that I can't mess up God's plans. Amen.**

Jesus,

In the Bible, a man named Job tried to understand why bad things were happening to him. He tried to explain it all to his friends too. But in the end, when God spoke to Job, Job realized how much he did not know—especially compared to God, who knows such wonderful things (Job 42:3)! **Jesus, help me remember that even when I don't know—God does! Amen.**

Dear Jesus,

In the Bible, one writer did not understand why he was going through such a hard time (Psalm 42:11). But he decided he would still praise God. Help me to have that same attitude. **Jesus, help me pray to God and praise Him, even when I don't understand everything. Amen.**

Jesus,

The Bible tells about a man named Gideon. God asked him to fight a mighty army. But Gideon did not understand. He was the youngest kid, in the smallest family. How could he be the one God wanted to lead an army? But through Gideon, the people saw God's mighty power (Judges 6–7). Wow! **Jesus, when I don't understand, help me follow God's better plan. Amen.**

Jesus,

The Bible says Mary and Martha didn't understand why You didn't come to heal their brother, Lazarus, when he was sick. Lazarus died, and everyone was sad. But because of this, You were able to show that God could do even more than heal the sick. He could raise the dead too (John 11)! **Jesus, I'm so thankful that Your power can do anything! Amen.**

Jesus,

When I don't understand, sometimes I get nervous. Sometimes I get scared. But the Bible tells me that in times like those, I can look to You and talk to You. You can make me feel better and make me happy when I don't understand (Psalm 94:19). **Jesus, when I'm nervous and don't understand things, remind me to talk to You. Amen.**

Jesus,

When I am having a hard time, when I just don't understand, help me to remember the Bible. Help me to remember all the things that You know, all the ways that God is working for me, all the things that I will one day understand. **Jesus, help me remember to pray to You whenever I don't understand.**
Amen.

When I Wonder about GOD

"Love the Lord your God with all your heart, with all your soul, and with all your mind." —Jesus

Matthew 22:37

Dear Jesus,

There is so much to know about God—so much that there's no way I could ever even begin to know it all! But even when I wonder, even when I'm learning, You remind me of the most important thing: I should try every day to love God with all my heart, all my soul, and all my mind (Matthew 22:37). **Jesus, help me to love God with everything I am. Amen.**

Dear Jesus,

Here's something I'm wondering about God: _____. I know that You already know the answer. Help me to understand. But I know that even if I learn the answer, I'll have so many more things I'll want to know about God. **Jesus, help me to always love learning about God. Amen.**

Dear Jesus,

When I look around, it's hard to think about how God created the whole world (Acts 4:24). The sparkling stars, the shining sun, the wispy clouds. The galloping horses, the snuggly puppies, the squeaky mice. Warm breezes. Falling leaves. Raindrops on my tongue. God created it all. And He created me. **Jesus, I am so grateful and amazed that God created the world—and me! Amen.**

Oh, Jesus,

God knows all the mysteries of the
world—things we wouldn't even
think of! In the Bible, God asked
Job if he knew where the snow
was stored, where rain came from,
or how to set the stars in place.
Of course he didn't! But God does.
**Jesus, help me remember that
God knows everything I could
ever dream to ask! Amen.**

Jesus,

When I wonder how long God has been alive—and will be alive—the Bible gives the answer: *forever* (Revelation 4:9). It's hard to understand how long that is, but I'm glad that it's true. **Jesus, I am really thankful that God will always be here. Amen.**

Jesus,

After a long day of running and playing, I am so ready for bed. But not God! The Bible says that God doesn't ever get tired (Isaiah 40:28). **Jesus, help me remember that when I am tired and weak, God is always going strong! Amen.**

Jesus,

Who is greater than God? No one!
When I think about how powerful
God is, it's amazing to realize that
no one and nothing is more powerful
than God. He is the great King (Psalm
95:3)! **Jesus, help me always
remember how mighty God is.
Amen.**

Dear Jesus,

The Bible says that God will rule "forever and ever" (Exodus 15:18). *Forever and ever.* That's a long, long time, much higher than I could ever count. **Jesus, I am so thankful to know that God will always be in charge, forever and ever. Amen.**

Jesus,

The Bible says that God is my safe place, that His arms hold me (Deuteronomy 33:27). That means the most powerful, all-knowing God who lives forever is holding me and keeping me safe. **Jesus, it makes me feel so safe to know that God is holding me. Amen.**

Dear Jesus,

A warm blanket, a big hug, a gooey chocolate chip cookie—the Bible says all good and perfect gifts are from God above (James 1:17). He is the Creator of all good and perfect gifts, like hugs and sunshine and fresh-baked cookies, and He loves to give them away. **Jesus, I am so thankful for all the gifts God has given me.
Amen.**

Jesus,

Sometimes I wonder . . . Does God get old? Does He get gray hair and wrinkles? Will He ever become mean and grumpy? Nope! The Bible says that God does not change (James 1:17). Everything else in this world may grow and change and get old and pass away, but not God. **Jesus, as I grow and change, help me to hold tight to the God who never changes. Amen.**

Jesus,

If I ever wonder if God would leave me, the answer is clear: NEVER (Hebrews 13:5). So many people will come in and out of my life, but not God. God will always be there. He will never leave me. **Jesus, it makes me feel so safe and loved to know that God will never leave me. Amen.**

Dear Jesus,

Sometimes I wonder what God is like. Does He like jokes? Does He love kittens? Is He quiet or loud? Even if I don't know the answers to *those* questions, the Bible is clear about one thing: God is love (1 John 4:8). And that sounds like a very good thing. **Jesus, help me always love learning about who God is. Amen.**

Oh, Jesus,

I love my parents and my family. I love my favorite stuffed animal. I love my friends and my home. But the Bible says that God loved us so much that He gave up the thing He loved most—His Son, Jesus—so that we could live (John 3:16). **Jesus, I am so thankful to be loved so much by God. Amen.**

Jesus,

Can I ever mess up so bad that God doesn't love me? The Bible says that even when people on earth were sinning, making choices that God did not like, He still sent His Son to give His life for us (Romans 5:8). **Jesus, help me remember that God loves me even when I mess up. Amen.**

Jesus,

The Bible tells me that God's love
never ends (Jeremiah 31:3). Never,
EVER! It's amazing to know that as
long as I live, all through eternity,
God will be right there, loving me.
**Jesus, I can't imagine anything
better than God's never-ending
love. Amen.**

Jesus,

In the Bible, God says we will find
Him when we look for Him with all
our hearts (Jeremiah 29:13). That
means when I wonder about God,
when I have questions, I can look
for Him, and He will be right there.
**Jesus, I am so grateful that God
is always there. Amen.**

Jesus,

Thank You for reminding me to love God with all my heart, soul, and mind (Matthew 22:37). Help me to always look for Him and to learn more about Him every day. **Jesus, more than anything, help me always believe in God's great love for me. Amen.**

When I Wonder about JESUS

"I am the way, the truth, and the life."—Jesus

John 14:6

Dear Jesus,

Thank You for making it very clear who You are. You are the way, the truth, the life for all of us (John 14:6). Everything we need, we can find in You. **Jesus, thank You for being my everything. Amen.**

Jesus,

Here's something I'm wondering about You: _____.
Help me to find the answer. Help me to understand. There is so much to learn about You. **Jesus, help me always to keep looking and learning more and more about You. Amen.**

Oh, Jesus,

The Bible tells us You were there with God right from the beginning (John 1:1). That's amazing! Everything God has seen, You have seen. From before creation to today and to eternity, You were there, You are here, and You always will be. **Jesus, thank You for always being there. Amen.**

Jesus,

You had a perfect home with God in heaven. And You left it to come to earth to be with us (John 1:14). While You were here, You taught people and healed people and gave Your life for us. You gave so much! **Jesus, thank You for giving Your life for me. Amen.**

Dear Jesus,

You are the Son of God (Luke 22:70).
When You were here on earth, many
people didn't believe You. They
couldn't believe that the Son of God
would actually come to earth as a
man. But I believe. **Jesus, I believe
that You are the Son of God.
Amen.**

Jesus,

Your friends, the disciples, saw You at work here on earth. They saw You teach the crowds and do miracles right in front of them. I can't imagine what it was like to live on earth with You back then, but I'm thankful I still get to talk with You now. **Jesus, thank You for being with me even today! Amen.**

Dear Jesus,

A long, long time before You came to earth, a prophet named Isaiah said that You were coming (Isaiah 9:6). He said that You would be called "Wonderful Counselor," "Mighty God," and "Prince of Peace." **Jesus, thank You for being all these things and so much more. Amen.**

Jesus,

It's hard to believe that You were once a kid like me. The Bible tells how You were born and how You grew, even how Your parents lost You once (Luke 2:45). Of course they found You in the temple, God's house, learning about Him. **Jesus, help me remember that You were once a kid like me, learning about God. Amen.**

Dear Jesus,

The Bible says that You welcomed children like me while You were here on earth. Even when You were busy, when the crowds were begging for Your time, You told Your friends to let the children come to You too (Matthew 19:14). **Thank You, Jesus, for always letting children come to You, back then and today. Amen.**

Jesus,

I know that You are perfect. And I'm not. I can be mean and selfish and grumpy and stubborn. But the Bible tells us that You didn't come to the world to tell us how bad we are. You came so that we could be saved (John 3:17). **Thank You, Jesus, for saving me.**
Amen.

Oh, Jesus,

The Bible tells us that You never sinned (Hebrews 4:15). You never made a bad choice. You never disobeyed Your parents or told a lie or took something from one of Your brothers. Thank You for Your example. **Jesus, help me to remember Your perfect example when I have a choice to make. Amen.**

Jesus,

You ask us to love each other the way that You love us, with lots of kindness and forgiveness and joy (John 13:34). Sometimes that can be hard! But You are such a perfect example of how we should love. **Jesus, help me to love others the way that You love me. Amen.**

Jesus,

When You left Your friends, Your disciples, here on earth, You gave them a job to do. You asked them to go into the world and tell everyone about You (Matthew 28:19). What a big, beautiful job, Jesus! I want to help. **Jesus, help me to do my job and tell everyone about You! Amen.**

Dear Jesus,

When You left this earth to go back to heaven, You sent a Helper, the Holy Spirit, to Your friends and to us. The Holy Spirit is here to guide us just like You did when You were here (John 16:13). **Jesus, thank You for sending me a Helper to guide me here on earth. Amen.**

Oh, Jesus,

I can't even begin to imagine the gift that You have given me with Your life. The Bible says that everyone who believes in You will have life forever (John 6:47). That means I can live in heaven with You one day, and that life will never end! **Jesus, I thank You and praise You for the gift of life forever with You. Amen.**

Jesus,

The Bible says that You are coming back to earth one day. When You do, You will come with great power and glory. And we all will see You (Matthew 24:30). It will be amazing! **Jesus, thank You for giving us such a wonderful day to look forward to!**

Amen.

Dear Jesus,

The Bible tells us that You never change. You are the same yesterday, today, and forever (Hebrews 13:8). A lot of things change around me—new teachers, new friends, new things to learn. Help me to remember that You never change. **Jesus, I know I can depend on You to stay the same forever. Amen.**

Jesus,

I love talking to You and learning about You. But I still feel like there is so much more to know. Even when I wonder, help me to remember who the Bible says You are. **Jesus, help me always love following and learning about You. Amen.**

When I Wonder about the BIBLE

"My words will never pass away."—Jesus

Mark 13:31

Dear Jesus,

In the Bible, one writer said that the Word of God was a lamp for his feet and a light that shined on his path (Psalm 119:105). It makes me think of a flashlight I could use when I need to know where I'm going in the dark. **Jesus, help me to use the Bible to light the path You want me to walk. Amen.**

Jesus,

Your Word tells us that the Bible was breathed out by God (2 Timothy 3:16). I imagine someone's foggy breath on a cold day—maybe that's like God's holy breath creating the Bible. When I don't know what to do, when I feel like God is far away, help me to remember to pick up my Bible. **Jesus, help me to remember that the Bible is the breath of God. Amen.**

Jesus,

The Bible says that when You were in the wilderness, hungry and alone (Matthew 4), Satan tried to tempt You to do something You shouldn't. You stopped Him with only the Word of God. That's how powerful the Bible is. **Jesus, help me to remember the power of the Word of God. Amen.**

Jesus,

When You talked about the Bible, You said that it is truth. When we need to know what is true and right, we know where to go. And when we read the words written in the Bible, we can know one thing for sure: they are true. **Jesus, thank You for the truth found in Your Word. Amen.**

Jesus,

When I get hungry, I know I need some food! But You said that humans need more than food to stay alive (Matthew 4:4). We need God's Word to feed our minds and souls just as much as we need food to feed our tummies. **Jesus, help me to be hungry to read the Bible and to feed myself with its truth. Amen.**

Dear Jesus,

I've watched leaves fall off trees. I've seen grass turn dry and brown. I've seen flowers fade and lose their petals. But the Bible says that God's Word doesn't pass away like those things do. The Bible will stand forever (Isaiah 40:8). **Jesus, thank You that Your Word, which is truth, lasts forever and ever. Amen.**

Oh, Jesus,

Help me to remember that the words You have given me aren't just words. You said that they are spirit and life (John 6:63). They help me grow closer to You, and, when I obey them, they help me have the best life. **Jesus, help me always to learn from the Bible so that I will have Your spirit and life. Amen.**

Dear Jesus,

The Bible has a lot of stories about a lot of people. But the Bible isn't just a bunch of stories. It teaches us the right way to live and shows us how much God loves His people. The Bible says that God's Word is much more than stories—it can save us. **Jesus, thank You for giving me Your powerful, saving Word. Amen.**

Jesus,

The Bible tells us how important it is to keep God's Word close. It says to keep God's words in our hearts, to take the words of the Bible with us everywhere we go (Deuteronomy 6:6–9). One way I can do that is by memorizing verses from the Bible and teaching my heart and mind to remember them. **Jesus, help me remember Bible verses so that I can keep them with me wherever I go! Amen.**

Dear Jesus,

The Bible tells us to put on the armor of God, a special kind of armor that protects us and helps us stay strong as our faith grows (Ephesians 6:10–17). The Bible is one piece of that armor. It's called the sword of the Spirit. I can use the words of the Bible to fight when I'm tempted to make bad choices. **Jesus, help me use God's Word to fight anything bad that comes my way. Amen.**

Jesus,

The Bible reminds us that when we keep God's Word in our hearts and minds, it helps us to make good choices (Psalm 119:11). It helps us to know right from wrong. **Jesus, help me keep God's Word in my heart so that I will make good choices. Amen.**

Dear Jesus,

It is so important to know God's Word. But *doing* what it says is even more important (James 1:22). This is hard, **Jesus. I need Your help! Help me, Jesus, to know God's Word *and* do what it says. Amen.**

Oh, Jesus,

Sometimes I get worried or scared or sad. But Your Word says that the Bible gives us hope (Romans 15:4). As I learn from Your Word, help me to hear and remember the stories and verses that will help take away my worries and fear and sadness. **Jesus, thank You for filling the Bible with hope! Amen.**

Dear Jesus,

You taught us that when we hear Your Word and do what it says, we will be blessed (Luke 11:28). That sounds easy! When I want to know the right thing to do, I can do what the Bible says, and my life will be blessed. **Jesus, help me to keep learning and doing what the Bible says. Amen.**

Oh, Jesus,

The Bible is so many things. It is stories of God's people. It is stories of God's love. It is a guide to living a good and Godly life. It is hope when I need it. **Jesus, thank You for giving me the Bible to depend on all my life! Amen.**

When I Wonder about HEAVEN

"There are many rooms
in my Father's house. . . .
I am going there to prepare
a place for you."—Jesus

John 14:2 ICB

Dear Jesus,

You told Your friends here on earth that You were going to make a home for them in heaven. People on this earth have been looking forward to heaven ever since! **Jesus, thank You for thinking of me and making me a home in heaven where I will live with You forever. Amen.**

Dear Jesus,

Here's something I would
love to know about heaven:

_____. I know
You know the answer. I know You
are there and have seen heaven for
Yourself. I know You know it as well
as I know my own home. **Jesus,
help me to keep searching for
answers about heaven. Amen.**

Oh, Jesus,

You said that heaven is "paradise" (Luke 23:43). I can't even imagine how beautiful that must be. I like to think about the colors and the sounds and all the amazing parts of heaven. I can't wait to see it and walk around it with You! **Jesus, thank You for creating a paradise for me to live in forever. Amen.**

Jesus,

There is a lot of sadness on this earth. But the Bible says that in heaven there will be no death or crying or pain. Heaven won't have any hospitals or funerals, and no one will ever have to say goodbye. God will wipe all the tears from our eyes (Revelation 21:4). **Jesus, I am so thankful that the sad parts of this world will not be in heaven. Amen.**

Jesus,

The Bible says that we won't be hungry or thirsty in heaven. I get hungry and thirsty sometimes, but then I think of all the children around the world who don't have enough food to eat or clean water to drink. They are hungry and thirsty *all* the time. Heaven will be such a wonderful place for them. **Thank You, Jesus, that one day, we will never be hungry or thirsty again. Amen.**

Wow, Jesus,

You say that in heaven, there are many rooms in Your Father's house. I can count the number of rooms in my house here on earth, but I'm guessing the number of rooms in heaven is a whole lot more. I just can't imagine how big heaven will be. **Jesus, thank You for building a house with a room just for me. Amen.**

Oh, Jesus,

Heaven sounds like such a beautiful place. The Bible says that it has a crystal-clear river filled with the water of life. Bright green trees, full of colorful fruit, line the sides of the river. I love trying to imagine it, but I know it is more beautiful than anything I could ever dream. **Jesus, thank You for creating a heaven more beautiful than I can imagine. Amen.**

Jesus,

In heaven, no one will be worried about having enough money. The gates are made of pearls, the walls and buildings are shining jewels, and the streets are made of solid gold. **Jesus, help me to remember that the worries of this world will have no place in heaven. Amen.**

Oh, Jesus,

When we get to heaven, it will be like a big party! We will get to see people we lost on earth (1 Thessalonians 4:17). It's really hard when we lose people, but if they followed You, we get to see them again one day. They are waiting for us in heaven. **Jesus, thank You for all the people I'll see again in heaven! Amen.**

Jesus,

When I think about the people who are waiting in heaven, this is who I want to see the most: _____. There are so many questions I want to ask them. And I just want to give them a great big hug. **Jesus, please tell them hello and that I can't wait to see them. Amen.**

Wow, Jesus,

The Bible says that in heaven, every language and nation from all over the world will come together and praise You. What an amazing sound that will be! And what a beautiful sight that will be! **Jesus, I can't wait to stand with the whole world, singing songs to You! Amen.**

Dear Jesus,

There are a lot of times when I've been really happy, and there are a lot of things that bring me joy. Thank You for each of them. But in heaven I'll have a joy that's bigger than anything, because God will be there with me (Psalm 16:11). **Jesus, I can't even imagine the joy that's waiting for me in heaven. Amen.**

Oh, Jesus,

The Bible says that in heaven, there will be thousands and thousands of angels (Revelation 5:11)! What will that look like? What will that sound like? What will that feel like? **Jesus, I am so thankful that one day I will see the angels in heaven. Amen.**

Jesus,

Here on earth, things run out.
Things break down. Things wear
out and get old and dirty. But in
heaven, that won't happen. You are
making everything sparkly and new
(Revelation 21:5). **Jesus, thank
You for making everything new!
Amen.**

Dear Jesus,

The Bible says that heaven won't need lights. It won't even need the sun. All of heaven will be lit by God's glory (Revelation 22:5). I can't really picture how that works or what that means, but I know it will be beautiful. **Jesus, I am so excited to one day stand in the middle of God's light! Amen.**

Jesus,

Some days are hard. I get hurt or sad. I feel sick or get angry. Those days seem far away from God's joy. But thinking about heaven makes me happy and full of hope (1 Peter 1:3–4). I can face the hard days bravely when I remember that one day, I will be with God forever. **Jesus, thank You for the hope that heaven brings. Amen.**

Jesus,

Right now, the home where
I live is in this city and state:
_____. But if I
believe in You and follow You, my
forever home is in heaven, with You
(Philippians 3:20). **Jesus, thank You
that my forever home is with
You. Amen.**

Dear Jesus,

I want to live with You forever in heaven someday. Jesus, I believe in You. I know You gave Your life to forgive me of my sins. Please forgive me. **Jesus, I want to follow You all my life, all the way to heaven. Amen.**

Oh, Jesus,

It has been so wonderful having all these little talks with You. On the glad days and the sad days, any day is happy and full of hope because You are in it. I don't want our talks to ever end. **Jesus, I want to talk to You and learn from You all the days of my life. Amen.**